To our friend Jean
Love Mom? &
Sharon

Law of
ATTRACTION

The Science of Attracting More of What You Want
and Less of What You Don't

Michael J. Losier

Dream Big
Michael Losier

Published by Michael J. Losier
Victoria, BC, Canada
Second printing

Publisher: Michael J. Losier
Illustrations/Artwork: Steve Flora, Flora Grafix
Cover & Layout: Reber Creative
Copy Editor: Maria Lironi, Cat's-Paw Communications
Proofreader: Deborah Wright, Precision Proofreading

ISBN: 0-9732240-2-9

Contact information:
Michael Losier
#110-777 Fort Street
Victoria, B.C., Canada
V8W 1G9
michael@michaellosier.com

Printed in Canada

Table of Contents

What Others Are Saying About This Book

Michael Losier's message will change the way you view yourself and others. I found Law of Attraction *both inspiring and healing.*

Ethelle G. Lord, M.Ed., CCG
Teamwork Development Associates
www.teamworkcoaching.com

Michael Losier has a gift for being able to distill abstract principles into results that work. Law of Attraction *is easy to read, easy to apply, and best of all, it really works!*

Mary Marcdante, Speaker,
Author of *My Mother, My Friend*
www.marymarcdante.com

One of the most profound revolutions in our thinking concerns the fundamental connections between who we are and what we attract to us. Through his work, Michael Losier wisely shows us the blueprints for transforming these connections by teaching us how to easily and reliably attract what (and who) we want in our lives. We have been blessed by the publication of Law of Attraction—*Michael's groundbreaking, "must-have" book.*

Mark Charlton, Vital Signs Lifecards

Michael's book takes a potentially complex and philosophical topic and simply describes what action you need to take so that you can reap all the rewards the Universe is holding for you. My business life has turned into an exciting and profitable venture because of the easy steps Michael outlines in Law of Attraction.

Linda Schaumleffel
Facilitator, Personal Coach,
Speaker, TeleClass Instructor
www.lose-weight-for-a-lifetime.com

How the Law of Attraction Changed My Life

Before I learned about the Law of Attraction, I wasn't satisfied with my professional life. Stuck in a job that was going nowhere, I was given no opportunity to be creative. I worked long hours and had little time for outside interests. Even though I had a dream that could have motivated me to leave it, I didn't. I stayed in that job for eight long years because I needed an income.

Things changed, however, once I learned about the Law of Attraction. I started to recognize pursuits—such as coaching and teaching—that made me feel good. So I decided, "I need to do more of this." I used the Law of Attraction to gain more information and to attract opportunities to coach and teach.

Even though I was still working at my government job, within a year I had taught more than 50 seminars. By now I was close to living my dream—to spend my days teaching others about the Law of Attraction.

My dream was realized, but slowly. I managed to convince my employer to let me work just four days a week, which was a first for that employer. For the next five years I worked four days a week, then three days a week, while I concentrated on building my coaching practice. In 2000, I left my job and I've never looked back.

Now I am happy with my professional life. I've never felt so creative and alive. I'm also doing much better financially than I ever did when I worked for someone else. Plus—I call the shots.

People are always asking me why my life is so great. So I tell them this story, and how understanding and using the Law of Attraction made it all possible.

Often their next comment is, "You should write a book."

So here it is, your own how-to guide for using the Law of Attraction to improve your life.

Here's to your success!

Michael

You're Already Experiencing the Law of Attraction

Have you noticed that, sometimes, what you need just falls into place or comes to you from an out-of-the-blue phone call? Or you've bumped into someone on the street you've been thinking about? Perhaps you've met the perfect client or life partner—just by fate or being at the right place at the right time? All of these experiences are evidence of the Law of Attraction in your life.

Have you heard about people who find themselves in bad relationships—over and over again—and who are always complaining that they keep attracting the same kind of relationship? The Law of Attraction is at work for them, too.

The Law of Attraction delivers both what is wanted and what is unwanted. By reading this book, you'll come to understand why and how this happens.

There are a number of words or expressions that describe Law of Attraction experiences. Here are just a few:

- Out-of-the-blue
- Serendipity
- Coincidence
- Fate
- Karma
- Synchronicity
- Luck
- Meant to be
- Fell into place

In this book you'll learn why these experiences happen. More importantly, you'll discover how you can use the Law of Attraction more consciously. You'll be able to attract all that you need to do, know, and have, so you can get more of what you want and less of what you don't want. As a result, you'll have your ideal client, your ideal job, your ideal relationship, your ideal vacation, more money in your life, and all that you desire. Really!

Definition of the Law of Attraction

I attract to my life whatever I give my energy, focus, and attention to, whether wanted or unwanted.

The Science of the Law of Attraction

There is a physiological foundation for positive thinking and its effect in creating the Law of Attraction.

As you may recall from your high school science classes, there are many forms of energy: atomic, thermal, electromotive, kinetic, and potential. Energy can never be destroyed.

You may also recall that all matter is made up of atoms, and that each atom has a nucleus (containing protons and neutrons) around which orbit electrons.

Electrons in atoms always orbit the nucleus in prescribed "orbitals" or energy levels that assure the stability of the atom. Electrons may be compelled to assume "higher" orbits by the addition of energy, or may give off energy when they drop to a "lower" orbit. When it comes to "vibrations," if atoms are "aligned," they create a motive force, all pulling together in the same direction, in much the same way as metals can be magnetized by aligning their molecules in the same direction. This creation of positive (+) and negative (-) poles is a fact of nature and science. Suffice to say, science has shown that if there are physical laws that can be observed and quantified in one arena, there are most probably similar laws in other arenas, even if they cannot at this time be quantified.

So you see, the Law of Attraction isn't a fancy term or new-age magic; it is a law of nature that every atom of your body is constantly responding to whether you know it or not.

When it comes to your own energy, your vibrations (moods or feelings) are either positive or negative.

The Law of Attraction responds to whatever vibration you are offering, by giving you more of what you are vibrating. It doesn't decide whether it is good for you or not, it simply responds to your vibration.

Think about the expression, "He gives off good vibes." Each one of us gives off good or bad vibes. In fact, we are constantly vibrating. If you are excited, content, appreciative, or feeling gratitude or pride, then you are offering a positive vibration. If you are angry, sad, disappointed, or feeling poor, unlucky, or defeated, then you are sending out a negative vibration.

Vibrations (feelings)

Positive	Negative
joy	disappointment
love	loneliness
excitement	lack
abundance	sadness
pride	confusion
comfort	stress
confidence	anger
affection	hurt

It's important to be in touch with, and aware of, your vibration because whatever you're vibrating, the Law of Attraction will give you more of.

Non-deliberate Attraction

Most of the time, you are offering a vibration unknowingly. For example, observing something that brings you joy will raise your vibration and you, too, will vibrate joy. Conversely, if you observe something unpleasant, you will start to offer that same negative vibration.

Remember, the Law of Attraction simply responds to whatever you are vibrating by giving you more of that feeling.

Reality Cycle
(Non-deliberate Attraction)

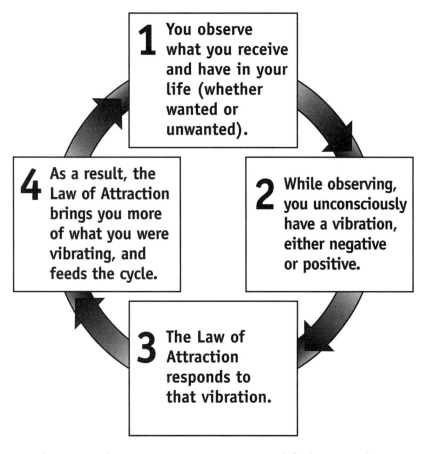

1 You observe what you receive and have in your life (whether wanted or unwanted).

2 While observing, you unconsciously have a vibration, either negative or positive.

3 The Law of Attraction responds to that vibration.

4 As a result, the Law of Attraction brings you more of what you were vibrating, and feeds the cycle.

Observing what you are receiving in your life, how much money you have, and the quality of your relationships, your work, and your health, comes with a feeling (vibration) that can be either positive or negative.

Even though you may not be aware of it, you are perpetuating the "reality cycle." The Law of Attraction will respond to your vibration, whether positive or negative, by giving you more of what you were vibrating.

In the next section, you are going to discover how to use the Law of Attraction more **deliberately**. To do this, you'll learn an easy, three-step formula. In addition to learning the steps, and following along with two case studies, I have provided blank worksheets so you can participate. More worksheets are available at www.LawofAttractionBook.com/worksheets.html.

The Three-Step Formula for Deliberate Attraction

Step 1. Identify Your Desire

You'll learn an easy script for accurately defining anything in your life. Once your desires are identified, it will be easier for you to vibrate more of what you really want.

Step 2. Raise Your Vibration

Discover how you can deliberately raise your vibration when using the "Desire Statement" tool. In other words, you'll learn how to offer a positive vibration for your desires.

Step 3. Allow It

Learn how to reduce and even eliminate the doubt and resistance that stops you from attracting what you want. This section is packed with tools that you will enjoy using over and over again.

Remember, whatever you are vibrating, the Law of Attraction will give you more of.

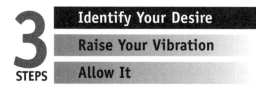

Step 1
Identify Your Desire

Words, Words, Words

Most of the tools and worksheets in this book are related to language, the use of words, and, most importantly, the feeling behind words.

Words are the common denominator for all three steps in the Deliberate Attraction process.

Why Is There Such an Emphasis on Words?

Words are everywhere. We speak them, read them, write them, think them, see them, type them, and hear them in our head. It's important to understand that all words carry a vibration for the person who says or thinks them.

In the following chapters, you'll learn about some very powerful words.

*The Law of Attraction responds the same way your mind does: it hears what you don't want. When you hear yourself make a statement containing the words **don't**, **not**, or **no**, you are actually giving attention and energy to what you don't want.*

Remember, you attract to your life whatever you give your attention, energy, and focus to, whether wanted or unwanted.

Don't, Not, and No

Your unconscious and conscious mind filters out the words **don't**, **not**, and **no**. Whenever you use these words, you are actually internalizing in your mind the exact thing you are being told not to. For example, if I said, "Do not think of a snowstorm," I guarantee that you would start thinking of a snowstorm almost immediately. Even though the instruction was to **not do** something, your unconscious and conscious mind edited out *that* part of the instruction.

There are other common expressions that give more attention and energy to what you don't want. Have you used or heard any of these statements?

Don't get mad.	Don't look now.
I'm not blaming.	Don't run with scissors.
Don't hesitate.	Don't forget.
Don't be fooled.	Don't litter.
Don't worry.	Don't smoke.
This won't hurt.	I'm not judging.
Don't panic.	Don't be late.
No rush, no worry.	Don't slam the door.

Declarative Statements

A declarative statement is an expression we use as a statement of truth. It can be positive or negative and is often made unconsciously.

Negative Declarative Statements

- I'll have to work hard to make good money.
- I never win the lottery.
- I'll never lose the weight I want.
- Good women/men are hard to find.
- Money comes in one hand and goes out the other.
- It's hard to get clients during the summer.
- I take one step forward and two steps back.
- My business slows down during the holidays.

Complaining and worrying are negative declarative statements. Every time you complain about something, you're giving more attention to what you don't like. When you worry about the future, you're giving more attention to what you don't want.

Positive Declarative Statements

- I'm lucky, because I always find money.
- I always find work and clients easily.
- Everything I touch turns to gold.
- I make friends easily.
- Money comes to me at the right time.
- I always get a great parking spot.

At this point, you're probably asking yourself how you can stop your pattern of negative thinking. The answer comes in the act of rephrasing what you think and what you say.

How to Rephrase a
Negative Declarative Statement

As you become more aware of your use of language and its importance in your vibration, you will begin to catch yourself whenever you make a negative declarative statement. When you hear it, turn the negative into a positive by restating what you have just said. Preface your sentence with "in the past." For example, if you hear yourself say, "It's hard to find clients," rephrase it by saying, "In the past, it was hard to find clients."

If you are curious about whether you are sending out positive or negative vibrations in any area of your life, simply take a look in that area and see what it is you are receiving.

It's a perfect match.

Clarity Through Contrast

What Is Contrast?

The first step in making the Law of Attraction work *for* you is to be clear about what you want. You can do this by first becoming clear about what you don't want. We call these "dislikes" **contrast**.

Contrast, as it applies to the Law of Attraction, is whatever does not feel good and puts you in a negative mood. The moment you identify something in your life that feels like contrast, and you spend time complaining about it, talking about it, or declaring that you don't want it, you are offering it to the Law of Attraction.

By observing the contrast, and identifying it as something you don't want, you become clearer about what you do want. Simply ask yourself, "So, if I don't want that, what do I want?" In other words, you'll find clarity through contrast.

Take your first boyfriend or girlfriend, for example. Chances are you're no longer with that person and because of that relationship you have a long list of things that you'll never put up with again. This is your list of contrasts. It is this list that will help you be clear about what you do want in a partner. In other words, when it comes to ex-boyfriends and girlfriends, observing contrast creates clarity.

*Observing contrast
is essential because
it delivers clarity.*

Why Is It Important to Identify Contrast?

You naturally experience clarity whenever you observe contrast in your life.

Imagine you are riding in your car with your best friend who insists on fiddling with the radio dial. For a brief moment the dial gets stuck on a heavy metal station—which you hate. You begin to feel stressed.

After five seconds of the music you say to yourself, "This is my car and I'm not listening to this for one second longer." You reach over and change the dial to your favorite station, which plays adult contemporary music. Instantly you feel happier and more relaxed.

Notice how you become clear about what you like by paying attention to what you don't like. In other words, your contrast has provided you with clarity.

Because the Law of Attraction is always responding to your vibration (whether wanted or unwanted), it is important to quickly take the focus off what you don't want (contrast) and redirect it onto what you do want (clarity).

Observe contrast briefly.

How Long Should I Observe Contrast?

The key to getting what you want, without getting stuck focusing on what you don't want, is to observe contrast briefly.

Only you can decide how prolonged briefly is. For some, experiencing contrast in a relationship may last for years; for others, contrast is observed for a short time. You might decide to end a relationship on the first date.

Notice that when you experience contrast around smells, sounds, or tastes, your tolerance is minimal. In other words:

How long would you smell something that doesn't smell good?
How long would you listen to music that doesn't sound good?
How long would you eat something that doesn't taste good?

In these cases, you are observing contrast and changing it to clarity, FAST.

There are, however, a few areas of your life where you may observe contrast for far too long:

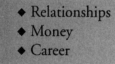

- ◆ Relationships
- ◆ Money
- ◆ Career

Generally, the least amount of time you spend putting your energy, attention, and focus toward contrast, the better. The Clarity Through Contrast Model, which you'll learn from this book, can help you with this.

A Clarity Through Contrast Success Story

In May, my client base had dwindled to zero (I was letting go of what I didn't want). By August, I had 12 clients and the kind of practice I wanted. The clients are exactly the kind of people I love working with. The two days that I had set aside for coaching were perfectly full, which gave me time for other things like developing retreats and writing a book. I got there, in part, by using the Clarity Through Contrast Model to identify what I really wanted and then created Desire Statements for my ideal practice and ideal clients. I raised my vibration by reading through the statements a few times and getting a real body feeling about how great it would be to have a perfect business and clients.

Jacquie Hale
Professional Personal Coach
Berkeley, California

The Clarity Through Contrast Model

The Clarity Through Contrast Model is a tool that will assist you in becoming clearer about your desires.

Here are some prominent areas in your life where clarity is beneficial:

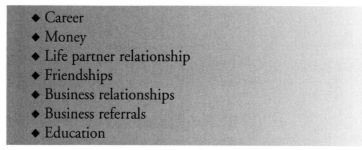

- ◆ Career
- ◆ Money
- ◆ Life partner relationship
- ◆ Friendships
- ◆ Business relationships
- ◆ Business referrals
- ◆ Education

Next, we'll examine two case studies that illustrate how the Law of Attraction can work for you.

Case Studies

After teaching the Law of Attraction to thousands of students, I've collected wonderful stories about people whose lives have been changed working with these ideas. And there's something about seeing someone else's story in print that really makes these ideas come alive. So I've chosen two case studies that represent two common areas where people use the Law of Attraction to get more of what they want.

Janice's story will show you how Identifying Your Desire, Raising Your Vibration, and Allowing what you want to come into your life can work in relationships. Greg's story focuses on another difficult issue for many people—money.

Janice—Relationships

Janice, 34, is tired and frustrated because she continually has the *wrong* kind of guy showing interest in her. She complains that she attracts men who are unavailable, insensitive, and who seldom make her a priority.

Janice decided to use the Law of Attraction to attract her ideal relationship.

She began the process of Deliberate Attraction with Step 1, Identifying Your Desire, using the Clarity Through Contrast Worksheet. Take a look at Janice's worksheet on the next page.

In Janice's case, she was able to build a large list of contrasts by recalling a number of past relationships and what she didn't like (contrasts) about those relationships.

Clarity Through Contrast Worksheet
Janice
My Ideal Relationship

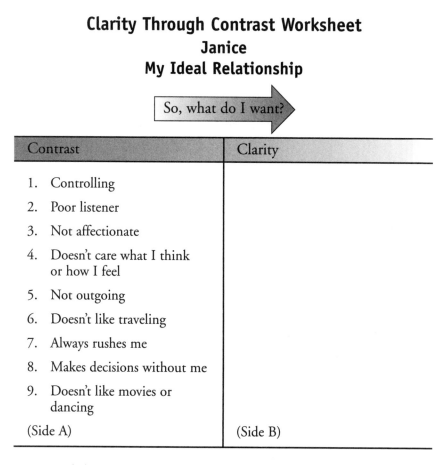

So, what do I want?

Contrast	Clarity
1. Controlling	
2. Poor listener	
3. Not affectionate	
4. Doesn't care what I think or how I feel	
5. Not outgoing	
6. Doesn't like traveling	
7. Always rushes me	
8. Makes decisions without me	
9. Doesn't like movies or dancing	
(Side A)	(Side B)

Janice made her contrast list on Side A. She recalled three past relationships during this exercise and took a couple of days to build her list.

Clarity Through Contrast Worksheet
Janice
My Ideal Relationship

So, what do I want?

Contrast	Clarity
1. ~~Controlling~~	1. Flexible, well-balanced
2. ~~Poor listener~~	2. Great listening skills
3. ~~Not affectionate~~	3. Affectionate, sensitive
4. ~~Doesn't care what I think or how I feel~~	4. Asks me what I think and how I feel about things
5. ~~Not outgoing~~	5. He likes to meet my friends and enjoys them
6. ~~Doesn't like traveling~~	6. Enjoys social situations. Loves short-term and long-term travel. Likes adventure and exploring new places together
7. ~~Always rushes me~~	7. Has patience. Allows things to unfold in due time
8. ~~Makes decisions without me~~	8. Asks for my ideas in decision making
9. ~~Doesn't like movies or dancing~~	9. Enjoys theater, movies, loves live bands and entertainment. Likes dancing
(Side A)	(Side B)

Janice read each item on her list and asked herself, "What do I want?" After she wrote the answer on Side B, she struck a line through the matching contrast.

Greg—Money

Greg, 27, is just making ends meet. He constantly complains about not having enough money. In fact, he says he's feeling stressed out about his financial situation. Greg is a self-employed consultant and business advisor and he's having a really hard time getting and keeping clients.

He has decided to use the Law of Attraction to attract his ideal financial situation.

The Deliberate Attraction process starts with Step 1, Identifying Your Desire, by using the Clarity Through Contrast Worksheet. Take a look at Greg's worksheet on the next page.

Remember, when it comes time to complete your own Clarity Through Contrast Worksheet, it may be helpful to recall a number of issues like Greg did in order to build a larger list of contrasts.

Clarity Through Contrast Worksheet
Greg
My Ideal Financial Situation

So, what do I want?

Contrast	Clarity
1. Not enough money	
2. Always bills to pay	
3. Just making ends meet	
4. I can't afford anything I want	
5. Money flow is sporadic	
6. I never win anything	
7. I'll always make the same amount of money	
8. Money does not come easily in my family	
9. I always struggle to pay the rent	
10. Money issues stress me	
(Side A)	(Side B)

Greg made his contrast list on Side A. He recalled his entire financial picture in the last year and took two hours to build this list. (He could have taken days to complete the list if he had wanted to.)

Clarity Through Contrast Worksheet
Greg
My Ideal Financial Situation

So, what do I want?

Contrast	Clarity
1. ~~Not enough money~~	1. Abundance of money
2. ~~Always bills to pay~~	2. Bills are paid easily and quickly
3. ~~Just making ends meet~~	3. Always have excess money
4. ~~I can't afford anything I want~~	4. Always have enough money to purchase whatever I desire
5. ~~Money flow is sporadic~~	5. Constant flow of money is coming in from multiple sources
6. ~~I never win anything~~	6. I win prizes often, receive gifts and many free things
7. ~~I'll always make the same amount of money~~	7. I am constantly increasing my monetary intake from known and unknown sources
8. ~~Money does not come easily in my family~~	8. Money comes easily to me
9. ~~I always struggle to pay the rent~~	9. Rent is paid easily, as I always have money
10. ~~Money issues stress me~~	10. Money and my relationship with it feels good
(Side A)	(Side B)

Greg read each item on his list and asked himself, "What do I want?" After he wrote the answer on Side B, he struck a line through the matching contrast.

Complete Your Own
Clarity Through Contrast Worksheet

Choose an area in your life you would like to change.

On Side A, list all of the things that are troubling you about your situation. For example, if you are building a contrast list about your ideal career, your list may include "the hours are too long" or "the pay is too low." Feel free to refer to a number of past jobs to help you build your list.

Take lots of time to complete this contrast list. Do it over a few days to ensure that you have thought of all the relevant episodes of contrast.

After you have completed building the contrast list on Side A, read each item and ask yourself, "What do I want?" and complete Side B of the worksheet.

By using this Clarity Through Contrast Worksheet, you will have a better understanding of what you do want (clarity of desire) by listing what you don't want (contrast). After you have reached clarity, simply cross off the matching contrasts.

Clarity Through Contrast Worksheet
My Ideal _____

So, what do I want?

Contrast	Clarity
List the things you don't like	List the things you would like
(Side A)	(Side B)

For more copies of this worksheet, go to
www.LawofAttractionBook.com/worksheets.html.

Clarity Through Contrast Worksheet
My Ideal _____

So, what do I want?

Contrast	Clarity
List the things you don't like	List the things you would like
(Side A)	(Side B)

At the end of this exercise, you'll have completed the first phase of Deliberate Attraction—Identifying Your Desire.

Remember, you've only pinpointed your desire at this point. You may have felt great about identifying and writing down what you wanted or you may have experienced a feeling of doubt.

In the following chapters, you'll learn ways to raise your vibration and make you feel more certain about obtaining your desire.

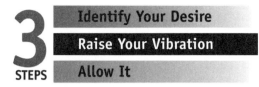

STEPS

Identify Your Desire

Raise Your Vibration

Allow It

Step 2
Raise Your Vibration

Increase Your Vibration

To raise (increase) your vibration simply means to give your moods or feelings more positive attention, energy, and focus.

It is not enough to merely identify your desire; you must also give it positive attention every day.

On the following pages, you'll find a few metaphors that will help you stay positive.

Choose to make all your decisions based on how they make your fan blow.

Blow Your Fan

If you think of your feelings as a fan then, when the fan is going full speed, you're feeling joyful. In other words, your "fan is blowing."

My fan is really blowing! This feels great.

When you experience a little irritant, you have a "pencil in your fan."

If it's more than an irritant, you have a "tree trunk in your fan." When you feel strong negative emotions—such as anger, fear, loss, or lack—your fan has stopped and you are not experiencing any joy. Rather, you are experiencing contrast or resistance. In other words, your fan has "shut down."

Oooh, that irritates me and puts a pencil in my fan.

Ask yourself, "How is my fan blowing?"

When observing the troubles of the day, spend less and less time giving them attention.

When I'm really angry, my fan doesn't blow at all. It feels like there's a tree trunk stuck in it.

You will come to love the metaphor of your fan blowing. You'll hear yourself say, "Ah, now that blows my fan!"

Identify what makes you feel good and do more of it.

What Is the Purpose of Your Life?

The purpose of life is to know and experience complete joy. Each person uses different strategies to experience joy.

An artist feels joy painting.
A singer feels joy singing.
A dancer feels joy dancing.

In these cases, painting, singing, and dancing are strategies for experiencing and feeling joy.

While reading this book, be open and willing to learn and uncover what would bring joy to you—in all areas of your life.

Realize that every vibration you offer creates your future. Become more deliberate about what you are vibrating. Begin to make decisions based on how things make you feel. Soon you'll be paying more attention to just how many negative feelings you are willing to tolerate. This is true self care.

Raising Your Vibration Fuels Your Desire

One of the keys to making the Law of Attraction work for you lies in keeping your desires at the forefront of your mind, thus giving them positive attention, energy, and focus.

In the next few pages, we're going to develop what I call a "Desire Statement." This is an effective tool for keeping your desires at the center of your attention. It is especially useful when dealing with new desires that may be forgotten if not given deliberate attention. That attention is given focus by a well-worded Desire Statement.

Why Using Affirmations
May Not Raise Your Vibration

An affirmation is a statement that, through the act of repetition, becomes implanted in your mind and reprograms your thinking. Most affirmations are spoken in the present tense. Saying "I have a happy, slender body" is an example of an affirmation.

Each time you read your affirmation, you'll have a reaction based on how the words made you feel. If, for example, you tell yourself that you have a happy, slender body when you do not, or when having a happy, slender body feels unattainable, you'll create negative vibrations. You'll offer a vibration of doubt, which the Law of Attraction will respond to by giving you more of what you don't want.

A Desire Statement is a much more effective tool for keeping your desire at the center of your attention and raising your vibration.

Most affirmations don't work because the Law of Attraction doesn't just respond to words—it responds to how you feel, too.

The Law of Attraction does not respond to the words you use or the thoughts you think.

It simply responds to how you feel about what you say and how you feel about what you think.

What is a Desire Statement?

A Desire Statement is an effective tool for raising your vibration and is the second stage in the three-step process of Deliberate Attraction. Once you're clear about what you want, writing a Desire Statement helps you stay focused on that desire. Remember, the more positive attention and energy you give your desire, the higher your vibration will be. The higher your vibration, the greater the likelihood that the Law of Attraction will match it by giving you your desire.

For example, you might say, "I want to own my own home." In that moment, the Law of Attraction is orchestrating circumstances and events to bring it to you. However, if you're like most people, you'll probably sabotage yourself by saying you can't afford your own home. Now you're telling the Law of Attraction that you can't afford it and you're stopping the energy flow. But you can keep the energy flowing by writing a Desire Statement.

Once you've written your Desire Statement, you should be experiencing feelings of excitement, possibility, and hope.

There are three elements to the Desire Statement: the opening paragraph, the body, and the closing paragraph.

Desire Statement—Opening Paragraph

I am in the process of attracting all that I need to do, know, or have, to attract my ideal desire.

Desire Statement—Body

Here are a number of phrases that you can use to express your desire:

E.g., "I love knowing that my ideal partner lives in my city."

I love knowing that my ideal _____
I love how it feels when _____
I've decided _____
More and more _____
It excites me _____
I'm excited at the thought of _____

The above phrases all use feeling words.

Can you feel the difference in vibration between:

I love knowing that my ideal relationship is nurturing and uplifting.
AND
My relationships are nurturing and uplifting.

In the first statement you're saying that your ideal relationship would be nurturing and uplifting, and this applies whether you're in one or not. Your vibration is positive.

The second statement is an assertion that you already have nurturing and uplifting relationships. If that isn't your reality, you'll vibrate doubt, which is a negative vibration.

Desire Statement—Closing Paragraph

The Law of Attraction is unfolding and orchestrating all that needs to happen to bring me my desire.

Before you write your own Desire Statement, let's look at the examples for Janice and Greg. Remember, Janice and Greg's first step was to build a list of contrasts (dislikes) to help them become clear about their desires. I've included their Clarity Through Contrast Worksheets here.

Clarity Through Contrast Worksheet
Janice
My Ideal Relationship

So, what do I want?

Contrast	Clarity
1. ~~Controlling~~	1. Flexible, well-balanced
2. ~~Poor listener~~	2. Great listening skills
3. ~~Not affectionate~~	3. Affectionate, sensitive
4. ~~Doesn't care what I think or how I feel~~	4. Asks me what I think and how I feel about things
5. ~~Not outgoing~~	5. He likes to meet my friends and enjoys them
6. ~~Doesn't like traveling~~	6. Enjoys social situations. Loves short-term and long-term travel. Likes adventure and exploring new places together
7. ~~Always rushes me~~	7. Has patience. Allows things to unfold in due time
8. ~~Makes decisions without me~~	8. Asks for my ideas in decision making
9. ~~Doesn't like movies or dancing~~	9. Enjoys theater, movies, loves live bands and entertainment. Likes dancing
(Side A)	(Side B)

To build her Desire Statement, Janice took her Clarity List and plugged it into the Desire Statement Model.

Janice's Desire Statement
My Ideal Relationship

Opening Paragraph

I am in the process of attracting all that I need to do, know, or have, to attract my ideal relationship.

Body

I love how it feels knowing that my ideal relationship is with a man who is flexible and well balanced. He has great communication skills and enjoys conversations.

I love how it feels knowing that my ideal partner is affectionate and sensitive and asks about my feelings. I love being asked to be included in decision-making opportunities.

I love knowing that my ideal partner enjoys and looks forward to meeting my friends in social environments. My partner and I enjoy short- and long-term travel together, experiencing trips and vacations that bring us closer.

I've decided that my ideal partner is patient, caring, gentle, and allows things to unfold in due time. It feels great to be asked by my ideal partner what I think and feel about things and to have balanced conversations where each of us is included. I love asking my partner for input and I love being asked.

I'm excited at the thought of enjoying the theater, movies, live entertainment and dancing with my ideal partner. I love being adored by my ideal partner and I love that my ideal partner enjoys being adored. He is optimistic and loves being uplifted. He's supportive and enjoys being supported.

Closing Paragraph

The Law of Attraction is unfolding and orchestrating all that needs to happen to bring me my desire.

Clarity Through Contrast Worksheet
Greg
My Ideal Financial Situation

So, what do I want?

Contrast	Clarity
1. ~~Not enough money~~	1. Abundance of money
2. ~~Always bills to pay~~	2. Bills are paid easily and quickly
3. ~~Just making ends meet~~	3. Always have excess money
4. ~~I can't afford anything I want~~	4. Always have enough money to purchase whatever I desire
5. ~~Money flow is sporadic~~	5. Constant flow of money is coming in from multiple sources
6. ~~I never win anything~~	6. I win prizes often, receive gifts and many free things
7. ~~I'll always make the same amount of money~~	7. I am constantly increasing my monetary intake from known and unknown sources
8. ~~Money does not come easily in my family~~	8. Money comes easily to me
9. ~~I always struggle to pay the rent~~	9. Rent is paid easily, as I always have money
10. ~~Money issues stress me~~	10. Money and my relationship with it feels good
(Side A)	(Side B)

Greg's Desire Statement
My Ideal Financial Situation

I am in the process of attracting all that I need to do, know, or have, to attract my ideal financial situation.

I love knowing that my ideal financial situation allows me to have and enjoy everything that I need and desire to bring more joy and freedom to my life.

Abundance is a feeling and I love the feeling of abundance all around me. I love knowing that all my bills are paid with joy, knowing that what I am billed for is an exchange, using money to honor that exchange.

I'm so excited at the thought of a constant flow of money coming to me from known and unknown sources.

I love knowing that my ideal financial situation brings me the comfort and the knowledge that I can travel where I want, shop where I want, and have whatever will make me feel great.

More and more, I receive gifts, win more prizes, and receive what I need from unknown and known sources.

I love the thought of stashing money away into excellent investments.

The Law of Attraction is unfolding and orchestrating all that needs to happen to bring me my desire.

How to Create Your Desire Statement

Now it's your turn to create your own Desire Statement.

Use the items on your completed Clarity Through Contrast Worksheet to build the body of your Desire Statement on the following worksheet.

I have provided you with the opening paragraph and ending paragraph. All you have to do is complete the body of the statement.

Use some or all of the following statements to help describe your ideal desire:

E.g., "I love knowing that my ideal job nurtures my creativity."

I love knowing that my ideal _____

I love how it feels when _____

I've decided _____

More and more _____

It excites me _____

I'm excited at the thought of _____

I love the idea of _____

It excites me to think about _____

There are two blank worksheets on the following pages. For more copies, go to www.LawofAttractionBook.com/worksheets.html.

Desire Statement Worksheet

Desire Statement
My Ideal _____

I am in the process of attracting all that I need to do, know, or have, to attract my ideal _____

_____

_____

_____

_____

_____

_____

_____

_____

_____

_____

The Law of Attraction is unfolding and orchestrating all that needs to happen to bring me my desire.

Desire Statement Worksheet

Desire Statement
My Ideal _____

I am in the process of attracting all that I need to do, know, or have, to attract my ideal _____

_____

_____

_____

_____

_____

_____

_____

_____

_____

_____

The Law of Attraction is unfolding and orchestrating all that needs to happen to bring me my desire.

How Do I Know If I'm Doing It Right?

After you've written your Desire Statement, go back and read it. Then ask yourself how you feel. Do you hear a little negative voice or have an uncomfortable feeling? Does your Desire Statement make you feel great? If not, then revise your statement so that you feel better when you read it.

Now, some of you may be saying: "I've had desires in the past that I got excited about and they never resulted in anything." Remember, Deliberate Attraction is a three-step process.

You've identified your desire and raised your vibration. The third step in the Deliberate Attraction process is Allowing. Let's get started.

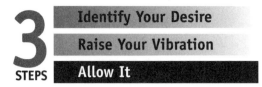

Step 3
Allow It

What Is Allowing?

In Law of Attraction terms, "Allowing" is simply the absence of doubt. It is the most important element in the Deliberate Attraction process. One of my clients, Danny, asked me why he did not attract his desires. He had built a great Clarity List of his ideal clients and made an awesome Desire Statement that felt great. So why didn't he attract his desires?

The process didn't work for him because it was not enough to just identify his desire and really want it. He also had to remove any doubt surrounding his belief that he would attract it. This doubt-removing process is called Allowing.

You may have heard the expression "just allow it." But telling yourself this does not make it happen. If you doubt you can have something, then you are not Allowing it.

You know you are Allowing something when you hear yourself say: "Ah, what a relief; this is possible."

I find Allowing is the most difficult step for most people. First of all, they don't understand its definition. Second, they become frustrated when people say, "just allow it." In this section, I'll give you the tools to overcome both of these obstacles.

Allowing is the absence of doubt.

The Allowing Game

The importance of Allowing is illustrated by a simple children's game.

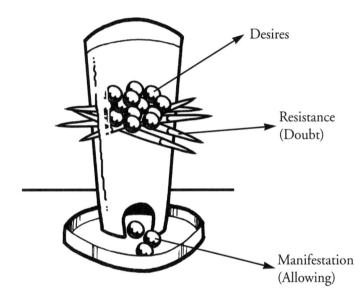

Desires

Resistance
(Doubt)

Manifestation
(Allowing)

Here's how the game works. A number of marbles rest on sticks that criss-cross through a clear cylinder. The sticks represent resistance (doubt), the marbles represent desire, and the fallen marbles represent manifestation (Allowing).

In the course of the game, the sticks are removed, allowing some marbles to fall to the bottom of the cylinder.

As you can see in the diagram, the only way the marbles will fall is if the sticks are removed. In the same way, having a strong desire and raising the vibration is not enough—it is only when your resistance is removed that your desire is manifested. And the faster your resistance is removed, the faster your desire can be realized.

In other words, the speed at which the Law of Attraction responds to your desire is in direct proportion to how much you allow.

The Power of Allowing

Having a strong desire with strong doubt means your desire will not be realized.

Having a strong desire with just a little bit of doubt means your desire will come, though slowly.

Having a strong desire with no doubt means your desire will be actualized so quickly that it'll knock your socks off!

The speed at which the Law of Attraction manifests your desire is in direct proportion to how much you allow.

If you have a strong desire but lots of doubt,
your desire will never come to you.

Where Does Doubt Come From?

The most common source of doubt is from your own limiting beliefs.

What is a Limiting Belief?

A limiting belief is a repetitive thought that is preventing you from attracting your desire. Your thoughts can send out a negative vibration. For example, the phrase "you have to work hard to make money" vibrates lack, which stops you from getting what you want.

Examples of limiting beliefs are:

- ◆ I don't deserve that.
- ◆ People gain weight after quitting smoking.
- ◆ It's hard to lose those last 10 pounds.
- ◆ You only get one chance in a lifetime.
- ◆ A perfect partner only comes along once.
- ◆ All the nice men are taken.
- ◆ All the nice women are taken.

The great thing about thoughts, however, is that they can be changed.

In this chapter, you'll learn how to use tools that will assist you in changing your limiting beliefs.

Allowing Statements

There are a number of tools for Allowing. The first one we're going to explore is Allowing Statements. The purpose of Allowing Statements is to lessen or remove any doubt that is preventing you from receiving what you want. After making your Allowing Statements, you should experience a feeling of confidence. That is, you know you really are going to attract what you desire.

Allowing Statements Really Work—A True Life Story

My two biggest Allowing Statements have to do with starting my business up from ground zero and marrying an exceptional (for me) man. Now that my desires are being manifested, I've come to believe that part of Allowing is recognizing and accepting that everything is leading to what I want, including things I wouldn't have guessed. Often that means eliminating some of what I already have. Now I find that when something not so great happens, I'm just soaring over it, not taking the thing so seriously, realizing it's all part of getting there! It feels like Christmas Eve. Because of it, every day I'm happy. And I haven't even completely reached where I want to be yet! Talk about raising your vibration!

Dr. Robin Lane
Psychotherapist, Coach, Private Instructor
Gouldsboro, Maine
www.selfesteemu.com

Allowing is the absence of doubt, and doubt is often created from limiting beliefs.

A limiting belief is a repetitive thought that prevents you from attracting your desire.

Formula for Creating Allowing Statements

Writing your own Allowing Statements is simple.

- ◆ Start by asking yourself if there is anyone currently doing what you want to do or having what you want. If so, then how many people have been doing this today? Yesterday? Last week? Last month? Last year?
- ◆ Write your statements in the third person because making reference to yourself only creates more doubt.
- ◆ Ensure that the statements are plausible.

Here is an example of the process at work when a single man doubts he can find a mate in his own city:

Question: Is there anyone on the planet who has attracted their ideal partner in their home city?

Answer: Yes.

Question: If so, then how many people have been doing this today? Yesterday? Last week? Last month? Last year?

Answer: It is possible that thousands of people found their ideal partner in their home cities last year and that thousands will find them in their home cities this year.

Examples of Allowing Statements:

- ◆ Thousands of people found their ideal partner in their home cities last year.
- ◆ Thousands of people will find their ideal partner in their home cities within the next six months.
- ◆ Every day more and more people are attracting their perfect mates in their home cities.

Now, let's return to Janice and Greg to see how they formed their Allowing Statements.

As you'll recall, Janice is tired and frustrated because she continually has the wrong kind of man showing interest in her. She complains that she attracts men who are unavailable, insensitive, and who never make her a priority.

Janice is using Deliberate Attraction to help her attract her ideal mate. She is clear about her desires and is already using a Desire Statement. Because this is a new desire for her, she has to lessen the doubt in order to receive it. She does this by composing Allowing Statements.

Janice's Allowing Statements
My Ideal Relationship

◆ Thousands of people met their ideal mate last month.
◆ Thousands of people are on first dates today with a person who will become their lifelong ideal partner.
◆ Hundreds of thousands of couples are enjoying each other's company today.
◆ Millions of couples are in their ideal perfect relationship.
◆ Every day more and more people are attracting their perfect mates.
◆ Millions of couples are doing social activities together including travel and vacations.
◆ Millions of couples will go dancing this week.

As Janice reads her Allowing Statements, she begins to feel hope and the reduction of doubt. Now, the Law of Attraction can bring Janice her ideal mate.

Remember Greg? The self-employed consultant and business advisor who's having a really hard time making ends meet. He constantly complains about not having enough money. In fact, he says he's feeling pretty stressed out about his financial situation.

Greg is using Deliberate Attraction to help him attract his ideal financial situation. He is clear about his desires and is already using a Desire Statement. Because this is a new desire for him, he has to lessen and remove the doubt in order to receive it. He does this by composing Allowing Statements.

Greg's Allowing Statements
My Ideal Financial Situation

- Millions of people are receiving checks today.
- Every day, billions of dollars are moved from bank account to bank account.
- Someone just received a check this minute.
- Hundreds of thousands of people win prizes and money every day.
- Somebody became a millionaire yesterday.
- Millions of dollars are inherited every day.
- Someone found money today.
- More and more people are attracting creative ways to bring in extra income.

As Greg reads his Allowing Statements, he begins to feel hope and the reduction of doubt. Now, the Law of Attraction can bring Greg his ideal financial situation.

How to Create Your Own Allowing Statements

It's time for you to use the first Allowing tool—the Allowing Statement. You can use the Allowing Statements Worksheet on the next page to help build your Allowing Statements.

STEP 1

Reread your Desire Statement and take information from it to plug into the Allowing Statements Model.

STEP 2

Start by asking yourself whether there is anyone currently doing what you want to do or having what you want to have. If so, then how many people have been doing this today? Yesterday? Last week? Last month? Last year?

STEP 3

Write your statements in the third person because making reference to yourself only creates more doubt. Ensure that the statements are plausible.

Here are more examples of Allowing Statements:

- ◆ Millions of people have jobs they love.
- ◆ Millions of people are working in careers where their creativity is nurtured.
- ◆ Millions of people are balancing their private lives with their professional lives.

Allowing Statements
My Ideal _____

_____

_____

_____

_____

_____

_____

_____

_____

_____

_____

_____

For more copies of this worksheet, go to
www.LawofAttractionBook.com/worksheets.html.

Now What Do I Do?

Now that you know how the Allowing process works, here are some tools that can improve its facilitation.

No matter which tool you choose to use, remember that Allowing is the absence of doubt. When you hear yourself say: "I know it's coming, I can feel it in my bones. I can clearly see myself having that," then you're experiencing Allowing.

Other Tools for Allowing and Raising Vibration

Index of Tools

1. Appreciation and Gratitude
2. Record Your Evidence of the Law of Attraction
3. Celebrate the Closeness of the Match
4. Use the Expression, "I'm in the Process"
5. Use the Expression, "I've Decided"
6. Use the Expression, "Lots Can Happen"
7. Ask for Information
8. Make Yourself an Attraction Box
9. Create a Void or Vacuum
10. Hold on to That Check
11. Allow the Law of Attraction to Figure It Out
12. Support and Resources

Appreciation and gratitude are the highest forms of vibration.

You can take time to admire anything. It's the feeling that's attached to your appreciation that is important.

Tool #1: Appreciation and Gratitude

Appreciation and gratitude are the highest forms of vibration. When you're appreciating something, you're offering a feeling and vibration of pure joy. Think of a time when you expressed thanks for someone in your life; the feelings you experienced were complete elation. In other words, you had no doubt or resistance.

An appreciation and gratitude journal is a helpful daily tool. Purposely taking time to treasure every day means that you are intentionally offering strong, pure, positive vibrations.

You can take time to admire anything. It's the feeling that's attached to your appreciation that is important.

Janice, whose desire is an ideal relationship, keeps a daily appreciation journal. It allows her to reflect on the relationships that she loves in her life. Here are a few samples of Janice's appreciation statements:

- I am grateful that I went hiking with new friends this week.
- I loved sharing over lunch today with close friends.
- I appreciate my close friends giving me their attention.
- I love having lots of friends.

While Janice is thinking and writing her daily appreciation statements, she is offering a vibration of appreciation. In that same moment, the Law of Attraction is unfolding to bring her more of what she is vibrating.

Tool #2: Record Your Evidence of the Law of Attraction

Keeping a diary or log of evidence of the Law of Attraction in your life will help you believe it more, get excited more, allow more, and trust more. Regardless of the size of the manifestation (e.g., you found a quarter or you won a prize), if it's something you desired—log it! Record your evidence and you will raise your vibration.

After a couple of pages of recording evidence, you will realize how much the Law of Attraction really is working in your life. As you use the Law of Attraction more knowingly, you will have confirmation that will help you trust the process of Allowing more easily, thus lessening the doubt (resistance). Remember, it's the absence of doubt that will bring your desire faster.

So, whenever you're feeling doubtful about the Law of Attraction, you just need to read your book of evidence. It will remind you how obedient the Law of Attraction is!

The Book of Evidence Worked for Ivor

Being analytically minded (I work in the financial business), I figured I was the most unlikely person to get involved with the Law of Attraction. But through Michael's teachings, I learned how to change my thoughts and be open and receptive to new ideas. Then wonderful things began to happen. I started taking an optimistic approach to business situations that I would generally worry about. When I deliberately raised my vibration from worry to a positive, happy mood, I noticed that I got results—and they came fast. If I decided I wanted to meet three new clients in one day, that's what happened! One of the ways I keep a record of how the Law of Attraction is working for me is I use a book to record all my successes, both big and small. I record if I was successful in getting a referral, a new client, paying off a bill or receiving a big check, etc. I refer to this log often—whenever I want to raise my vibration and remind myself how powerful the Law of Attraction is.

Ivor John
Financial Advisor
Victoria, BC

Remember, it's the absence of doubt that will bring your desire faster.

Tool #3: Celebrate the Closeness of the Match

Have you noticed how when something you desire starts showing up in your life—even just a little bit—it excites you? For example, you attract a bit of information you've been looking for, or you meet someone who is a pretty close match to your ideal partner or your ideal client. All of this is evidence of the Law of Attraction.

How you observe evidence of the Law of Attraction is important. In some cases, people might say: "Oh, this isn't exactly what I want." "He's not quite the right person I was looking for." "It's kind of close but not really." This is a negative vibration.

When you find and experience evidence of the Law of Attraction, celebrate it by acknowledging how close you came to getting what you wanted. It's in the celebration of the closeness of the match that you offer more vibration of what you desire and—at that moment—the Law of Attraction is responding to your vibration. Remember, the Law of Attraction does not care whether you are remembering, pretending, playing, creating, complaining, or worrying. It simply responds to your vibration. So, find evidence and rejoice.

Janice, who is using the Law of Attraction to attract her ideal relationship, is a great example of how this tool can be used to lessen doubt.

Remember, the Law of Attraction does not care whether you are remembering, pretending, playing, creating, complaining, or worrying.

It simply responds to your vibration.

So, find evidence and rejoice.

We cannot hold two vibrations at the same time.

Therefore, choose to make your vibration a positive one so that you'll get what you desire.

Shortly after Janice completed her Desire Statement and started using the Allowing tools, she met a man who was a visitor to the city. They hit it off right away. They had lots in common including a love of music, theater, and movies. She was really impressed by his good communication skills and how upbeat he was. In short, Janice's fan was blowing. Three days later, Janice called me and I could hear a pencil in her fan. She spent lots of time and attention on her disappointment that he was from another country. Yet, I knew he was a close match to her desire and also that she was no longer acknowledging that fact.

Here's how I used this tool with Janice—I simply asked her to tell me all the things about her new friendship that blew her fan, in other words, the things that made her feel great and were in her Desire Statement. She quickly built a list that included his great communication skills; his love of music, theater, and movies; his values; and how happy she felt around him. The moment Janice started creating this list, she could feel her vibration rise. Finding and celebrating the closeness of the match shifted her vibration immediately.

And you know how the Law of Attraction responds to that!

Tool #4: Use the Expression, "I'm in the Process"

Sometimes it's hard to believe you will get what you desire most. This is especially true if you're focusing on the fact that you haven't reached your goal. When you concentrate on what you don't have, you're offering a negative vibration. So instead, feel the relief of saying, "I'm in the process."

Saying you don't have something is another way of focusing on the lack and offering a negative vibration. Whenever you catch yourself saying you don't have something yet, stop and instead say, "I'm in the process of attracting."

Now, does that feel more believable? You're doing something. You are on your way.

- I'm in the process of attracting my ideal mate.
- I'm in the process of obtaining my ideal job.
- I'm in the process of learning more about the Law of Attraction.

Tool #5: Use the Expression, "I've Decided"

Another way to rephrase your expressions so they offer a positive vibration is to use the phrase, "I've decided."

"I'm in the process" or "I've decided" take the spotlight off lack and put it onto action. These phrases have a positive emotional charge to them. You'll feel relief when you decide something.

◆ I've decided I'm going to have more money in my life.
◆ I've decided I'm going to work three days a week.
◆ I've decided I'm going to be in a happy, healthy relationship.

Tool #6: Use the Expression, "Lots Can Happen"

I had a client, Jason, who was using the Law of Attraction to attract his ideal customer. I could hear in his declarative statements that he was trying to determine where his next major purchaser was coming from. He was saying things like, "I have to find a new contract" or "It seems like I've been waiting forever." Even though Jason had completed the entire three-step process, there was still a part of him that doubted. The declarative statements Jason was making about his next client had a negative vibration of lack (doubt).

Jason was spending a lot of energy trying to figure out why he wasn't getting what he wanted instead of trusting that his desire would come to him. Like Jason, you've probably spent some time noticing that you don't have everything you want. From now on, the moment you notice the lack of something in your life or hear yourself say, "I wonder when it's going to happen," remove the doubt by using the following Allowing phrase: "Lots can happen over the next few days."

You'll automatically feel relief from trying to determine how and when your desire will be realized. The moment I reminded Jason about the phrase, "lots can happen," I could see his relief. This experience also reminded him of times when lots happened without him trying to figure it out. Using this Allowing phrase helped Jason shift his vibration from lack to abundance, or from a negative vibration to a positive one.

Like Jason, the sooner you let go of how you think it needs to happen, or what you need to do to make it happen, the sooner the Law of Attraction can deliver it.

Remember, the speed at which the Law of Attraction responds to your desire is in direct proportion to how much you are Allowing.

Tool #7: Ask for Information

A first step in identifying your desire is to ask for information and ideas about that desire. Here's what I mean. Often when we define our desires and get excited about attracting them, the doubt we may have stops the Law of Attraction from bringing them to us. Try asking to receive information and ideas about your desire, because you will have less doubt in receiving it. If your desire is to have a full client base, for example, you may doubt that it is possible. However, you could desire to attract information that will help you with that goal. Try it. If you felt more hopeful after you asked for information, then you just reduced your doubts.

Feel like you've bitten off too much? Is your vision or goal overwhelming? Do you doubt your ability to receive it? Then maybe your desire needs to be broken down into smaller, more believable portions.

Remember, the Law of Attraction is a process. Divide the job into several segments by asking yourself:

◆ What do I need first to get started?
◆ What would be the ideal piece of information?
◆ What would be the ideal contact?

Smaller pieces feel more attainable. In most cases, you will feel less resistance because the things you need first are within reach.

One of the best techniques for breaking things down is the one I used with Greg's financial situation. Even after completing the three-step process, he still felt doubtful he could have what he desired.

Saying "lots can happen" will remind you that there are infinite possibilities as to when and how your desire will be manifested.

I asked Greg just to take the first step. That is, to accept any information that fit with his desire to receive more money. Greg instantly got excited and said, "Oh, what a great start! I can attract information about what I need to do to attract more money. That's what I need. Now, that I can do!"

Can you hear Greg's confidence and sense of relief that he can start the process?

Tool #8: Make Yourself an Attraction Box

An attraction box is used to collect things that represent your desire: things you've cut out of magazines and newspapers, brochures for trips you want to take, or even business cards of people you want to work with.

Your attraction box can be any type of container, as simple as a shoebox or as elaborate as a treasure chest.

Each time you put something into your attraction box, what you are actually offering, vibrationally, is hope, and hope is a positive vibration. Instead of throwing out the catalogues and the flyers and saying things like "I can't afford this" or "I'll never be able to have one of these," you now allow it, just a little. You do this because it's not your job to figure out where or when your desire is going to come. Just put it into your attraction box and leave the rest to the Law of Attraction.

Tool #9: Create a Void or Vacuum

A void or vacuum is always waiting to be filled.

As an example, let's say you're looking for more clients. By making space in your filing cabinet for new customers, even by labeling some empty file folders with their names on them, you are raising the vibration to attract new clients. Saying, "I'm waiting for new clients" or " I have only a few clients," can be rephrased as "I have room and space for new clientele." Do you hear how optimistic that sounds?

The key to creating this hungry void is to focus on the opportunity to be filled and concentrate on the emptiness of the hole. For example, when a client cancels, you can say you've just created a space to attract a new client.

Now, that's Allowing!

Abundance is a feeling.

Tool #10: Hold on to That Check

Do you want to raise your vibration when it comes to receiving more money? Then hang on to checks that you've received just a little bit longer.

Instead of cashing a check the day you get it, holding onto it will have more vibrational value if you observe it for a day or so. Every time you view the check, you will get a little jolt of excitement that will be offered to the Law of Attraction.

Abundance is a feeling. Do whatever it takes to raise your vibration and make you feel more abundant. Photocopy checks and put them in your wallet. Place crisp $50 bills on the shelf of your refrigerator and enjoy the rockets of abundance every time you open the fridge.

When you notice that something made you excited about money, do it over and over again. The Law of Attraction is always responding.

Your job is to be clear about your desire and to allow into your life whatever you need to manifest that desire.

Your job is not to try to figure things out intellectually but to let the Law of Attraction bring you the answers.

Remember, you get what you vibrate.

Tool #11: Allow the Law of Attraction to Figure It Out

Sometimes it can get a little overwhelming thinking about your desire and all that you need to do to obtain it. But you needn't be overwhelmed because the Law of Attraction will bring the answers to you.

At the very moment that you catch yourself saying:

◆ I don't know how to figure this out.
◆ I don't know where to look.
◆ I don't know how to find this information.
◆ I don't know what to do next.
◆ I'm having problems finding this.
◆ I can't figure it out.

Stop. Say to yourself, "That's not my job. I'm going to allow the Law of Attraction to figure this out."

This lesson was a valuable one for my client and friend, Andria. When she was first going into business for herself, she used the Law of Attraction to attract her ideal company. Using the three-step process, Andria discovered a business that really 'blew her fan' by allowing her to shop every day. She also used the Law of Attraction to find financing and the perfect location for her clothing consignment store. Through every step of the way, whenever the tough questions came up and Andria would worry about the details, I would say to her, "That's not your job. Let the Law of Attraction figure it out."

However, although the Law of Attraction took care of the big questions, Andria still had to do the follow-up actions. For example, after she found the name of the perfect banker, she still had to make an appointment to see him and arrange financing for her shop.

Tool #12: Support and Resources

Surrounding yourself with others who practice the Law of Attraction will help you to consistently offer a positive vibration. But how do you go about finding these people?

One way is to use the Deliberate Attraction process. Ask the Law of Attraction to bring to you people who would like to practice and master the art of Deliberate Attraction.

Another technique that I've experienced great success with is to place a little ad in a free weekly paper that reads, "The Law of Attraction Discussion Group. Contact Michael at michael@lawofattraction.ca." The ad cost me only $10 and I received numerous responses as a result of it. The same ad in the classified section of a local magazine should have a similar effect.

There are also a number of books, articles, and websites dedicated to the Law of Attraction. You'll find a list at www.LawofAttractionBook.com/resources.html.

Putting It All Together

Now that you've learned how to use the Law of Attraction to get more of what you want, and less of what you don't want, you can start using the techniques in this book right away.

At each step in the process, stop and listen to that little voice inside of you. Keep in touch with your feelings so you're always aware of what you are vibrating. Refer to this book often for guidance. You can also make use of other resources such as my classes on the Law of Attraction, one-on-one coaching, my monthly e-zine, and my website, www.LawofAttractionBook.com.

You now have the tools to let the Law of Attraction improve your life.

I wish you pure joy.

Michael

Acknowledgments
(in alphabetical order)

Danielle Allen
Mark Belford
Janit Bianic
Book Review Team
Geoff Gosson
Eva Gregory
Jacquie Hale
Rebecca Hanson
Marty Humphreys
Ivor John

Anna Kanary
Julia Kirchhoff
Maria Lironi
Mary Mitchell
Linda Storey
Murray Voss
Dory Willer
Simon Wills
Deborah Wright

A special thank you to everyone who has attended my Law of Attraction presentations, classes, and seminars—you've helped to create this book.

References

Abraham-Hicks Publications. www.abraham-hicks.com. 2002

Atkinson, William Walter. *Thought Vibration or the Law of Attraction in the Thought World.* Kila, MT: Kessinger Publishing Company, 1998 (1906)

Hill, Napoleon. *Think and Grow Rich.* Los Angeles, CA: Renaissance Books, 2001 (1960)

Wattles, Wallace D. *The Science of Getting Rich.* Pinellas Park, FL: Top of the Mountain Publishing, 1997 (1910)

Special Appreciation

Many of the concepts in this book come from Esther and Jerry Hicks of Abraham-Hicks Publications. It is with lifelong appreciation that I thank them for sharing their knowledge of the Law of Attraction with the world and with me. My life is fuller and richer because of it.

For more information about the Law of Attraction, visit Abraham-Hicks Publications at www.abraham-hicks.com.

About the Author

Business coach and author Michael J. Losier's career is a marriage of high-tech and metaphysics. After earning a diploma in business administration in 1990, Michael spent the next eight years working in information technology with the B.C. government. During this time he also started his own practice as a business success coach and trade show producer. Many clients, seminars, and trade shows later, Michael authored his first book, *111 Tips and Strategies for Successful Trade Show Exhibiting.*

In 1995, Michael's career took a dramatic shift when he started to study Neuro Linguistic Programming (NLP) and eventually earned a certificate in the subject from Progressive Edge Plus NLP. Soon after, Michael learned about the Law of Attraction and immediately set about deliberately applying its principles to his own life.

Now he teaches business courses on a variety of topics including the Law of Attraction through TeleClass International, which he co-founded in 1999.

When he's not teaching, leading, or learning, Michael enjoys hiking in old-growth forests of the Pacific Northwest and tending to his patio garden in Victoria, B.C.

Michael is available for private consultations, seminars, and speaking engagements. For more information, visit: www.LawofAttractionBook.com and www.TeleClassInternational.com.

Quick Order Form

Please visit www.LawofAttractionBook.com to see other
Law of Attraction products, including CDs and TeleClasses.

Fax orders (send this form):
Canada 1-250-380-9281
USA   1-413-691-5067

Telephone Orders: Call 1-877-550-9282 toll free
Online orders: www.LawofAttractionBook.com

Postal Orders: Michael J. Losier
                #110-777 Fort Street
                Victoria, BC Canada
                V8W 1G9

Name: _____

Address: _____

City: _____

Province/State: _____ Postal Code/ZIP: _____

Telephone: _____ Email address: _____

Sales tax: Canadian orders please add 7% GST.

Shipping in Canada and the US: Mailed within 24 hours;
shipping costs $3 US for the first book and $1 for each
additional book.

Book Price: $14.95 US / $21.95 CDN
Volume or reseller orders visit www.LawofAttractionBook.com
E-mail: michael@LawofAttractionBook.com

Payment:
☐ Money Order   ☐ AMEX   ☐ Discover   ☐ VISA   ☐ MC

Card number: _____

Name on Card: _____ Exp. Date: _____